Earn the Return
A Musician's Guide to
Getting Gigs & Being Invited Back

Chaye Alexander

For permission requests, contact:
Info@ChayeAlexander.com
ChayeAlexander.com

ISBN: 979-8-9933276-0-0

Printed in the United States of America
First Edition, 2025

Disclaimer
This book is intended for informational purposes only and does not constitute legal or financial advice.

Table of Contents

Foreword

by Letron Brantley, Jazz Saxophonist

I've known Chaye Alexander for nearly a decade, not just as a colleague in music but as a force who has shaped spaces with intention, elegance, and an uncompromising standard. To say she keeps it real would be putting it lightly. In a world that often settles for "good enough," Chaye has always demanded more of herself, her venue, and the talent that walks through her doors. Not for ego. Not for show. For the sake of integrity, excellence, and the sacred energy of live performance.

This book you are holding is not fluff. It is a masterclass in professionalism. It is the truth that too many artists wish they had heard earlier in their careers. *Earn the Return* is about more than getting booked. It is about being invited back because you respected the room, elevated the experience, and left a legacy that demands repetition. Chaye's insights come from hard-earned experience and a devotion to craft that is rarely seen but sorely needed.

If you are serious about longevity in music, if you understand that reputation travels faster than talent and lasts longer than applause, then you are exactly where you should be. Listen closely to what Chaye lays down in these pages. This is not just guidance. It is gospel for anyone aiming to move from gigs to greatness.

Let us raise the standard together.

Preface

This book is born out of decades of living, learning, and leading in music. For more than thirty years, I have worked both behind the scenes and in front of them, building spaces where artistry and excellence meet. Today, as the owner of Chayz Lounge, a boutique jazz venue known for its intimate setting and world-class performances, I handle all booking and production for the shows and am present for every performance. That means I have seen it all: the artists who rise to the occasion and those who fall short, the moments of brilliance that stay with an audience forever, and the missteps that can cut a career short.

Over time, I noticed something important. Too many talented musicians were missing opportunities not because of their music but because of what happened before and after the performance itself.

I wrote this book to share the lessons I have seen proven time and again. I wanted to give musicians the guidance I wish many of them had received sooner. This is not theory. It is not guesswork. It is the lived experience of booking, producing, and presenting shows night after night for artists at every level of their careers.

As a woman in a field largely dominated by men, I have been called the B-word, told I am too direct, and labeled difficult more times than I can count—usually by people who failed to meet the standard and did not like hearing it. I am fine with the name-calling because my expectations are high, and I make no apologies for asking others to rise to them.

I run a professional space where excellence is not optional and respect is non-negotiable. I take great care to ensure that every aspect of the Chayz Lounge is thoughtfully designed to create the best possible experience for our guests. I advocate for their comfort and for the integrity of the performance itself. That does not make me difficult. That makes me responsible.

This book is not filled with sugarcoating or lowered bars. It is written from lived experiences. It is for musicians who are serious about building something real and lasting. Although it may not cover every aspect of booking, performance, or the music business, it provides the essentials that determine whether you simply get on stage once or build a career that keeps you there.

Some points appear more than once, and that is intentional. The lessons that carry the most weight are worth repeating, because they are the very things that will make or break your reputation as a professional.

My hope is simple: these pages will help you understand what it takes not only to get booked but to earn the return. If even a handful of musicians take these lessons to heart and see the bigger picture, then this book will have served its purpose. Because in this business, longevity is built on more than talent. It is built on respect, preparation, professionalism, and relationships.

Introduction

Playing music is only part of the job. Getting booked and being invited back requires professionalism, preparation, and a clear understanding of how to work with venues and their audiences.

There is an old saying in the industry: *the music business is 10 percent music and 90 percent business*. It may sound exaggerated, but it is true. Success often depends on how well you handle contracts, communication, and reputation as much as how well you play.

This guide is built on more than advice. It is a collection of experiences, cautionary tales, and standards that separate amateurs from professionals. Here you will learn how to approach venues with the right mindset, negotiate with confidence, and deliver performances that leave a lasting impression.

At the core of these lessons is one truth: **success ON stage begins with how you show up OFF stage.**

Let's dive in, because the stage is waiting for you, and so is your chance to earn the return.

Before You Begin

Gigging Musician vs. Aspiring Professional Musician

The difference between a gigging musician and an aspiring professional isn't just talent. It is mindset, commitment, and strategic intention.

A gigging musician performs often and almost anywhere, sometimes even driving hours for a gig that pays only a few hundred dollars. They treat each show as a standalone event, focusing only on the moment rather than the bigger picture.

The aspiring professional sees every performance as a step toward building a lasting career rooted in branding, growth, and sustainability. They treat every gig not only as an opportunity to perform, but also as a chance to strengthen relationships, refine their craft, and position themselves for greater opportunities.

This guide is about making that shift — from gigging to growing. Because the goal isn't just to get booked. The goal is to build something worth booking.

As you read, ask yourself:
"Am I approaching this like a gigging artist, or like a future industry professional?"

Chapter 1: Preparing to Get the Gig

Practice as Preparation

There is a saying: *How do you get to Carnegie Hall? Practice, practice, practice.* It is not a joke, it is a roadmap. Every legendary stage has been graced by artists who understood that skill is not a gift, it is a discipline. The hours you put in when no one is watching show up loud and clear when everyone is.

Practice sharpens your timing, strengthens your delivery, and builds the confidence that audiences can feel. It is where you make mistakes, fix them, and ensure the music flows with ease long before you step on stage. A paying audience is not your rehearsal space, and a venue is not the place to work it out.

When your craft is rehearsed to the point of fluency, everything else you present becomes stronger because it rests on the foundation of being able to deliver musically at a professional level.

Aspiring Pro Mindset: Curate, Don't Just Send

Gigging musicians send whatever they have. Professionals curate. Every detail, from your photos to your sound quality to the way you speak about money, tells a venue who you are before you ever walk through the door. A sloppy email or low-quality demo can close doors faster than a missed note.

An aspiring professional understands that preparation goes far beyond music. It means thinking like a business. It means knowing what to send, how to send it, and what questions you must be ready to answer when a venue is interested.

If your materials do not reflect professionalism, neither will you.

Presentation is part of the performance. Before you ever play a note, you have already communicated your value through what you choose to send. An aspiring pro does not just throw these pieces together. They curate with intention, ensuring each element tells the same story about who they are and the experience they bring.

DO: Create a Professional EPK

Your Electronic Press Kit is not a formality. It is a strategic branding tool. A professional EPK should include:

- **Bio**: Concise and compelling, highlighting key achievements and qualities that separate you from the crowd.

- **Music Samples**: High-quality recordings that showcase your best work, preferably aligned with the type of venues you are targeting.

- **Live Performance Footage**: Nothing replaces this. Use clear video and clean audio so bookers can focus performance rather than shaky or muffled production.

- **High-Resolution Photos**: Images that match your brand and stage aesthetic.

- **Press Coverage**: Articles, interviews, or features that add credibility.

- **Contact Information**: Booking details, social media, website links, and management or agent contacts if applicable.

DO: Make Time to Practice Your Craft
This is not optional. It is the discipline that keeps your skills sharp and your confidence high. Saying you do not have time is another way of saying you do not value your craft. Filling your calendar with back-to-back gigs but never carving out time to rehearse means you are slowly eroding the very foundation of your career.

When you neglect practice, you are not just letting your skills slip. You are taking your God given gift for granted. Every talent needs care, discipline, and refinement. The moment you stop investing in it, you begin to lose the very thing that sets you apart.

DO: Build a Strong Online Presence
Your website and social profiles are often the first impression bookers will have. Treat them as your storefront. Make them clean, consistent, and reflective of your brand.

- **Website**: Keep it simple, mobile-friendly, and easy to navigate. Include your bio, music, videos, press, and contact information.

- **Social Media**: Update regularly with professional content that shows your performances, rehearsals, or creative process. Avoid clutter, drama, or personal content that distracts from your artistry.

Remember, a booker's first stop is often Google. What comes up should reinforce your professionalism, not call it into question.

DO: Know Your Numbers Before You Pitch
Preparation isn't just creative. It's financial. Research market rates, decide your minimum, and be ready to discuss it without hesitation. When a venue asks, "What is your fee?" you need a clear, confident answer.

Nothing undermines your credibility faster than stalling when asked about money. Do not wait until a contract is on the table to think about your rates.

Professionals establish a rate range that reflects the venue size, location, and event type. They also know how to scale by offering solo, duo, or full band formats depending on the budget.

You do not need to lock yourself into one number. Instead, present your value in tiers:

- A base fee for your standard performance.

- A higher fee for larger ensembles or special requests.

- A willingness to adjust if travel, lodging, or extended performance time is required.

Professionals prepare on every front: musically, visually, and financially. Being prepared with numbers shows you are serious. Hesitation, fumbling, or saying "I don't know" signals the opposite.

DO: Be Fully Ready Before You Reach Out
Make sure every element of your presentation is polished
and complete before contacting a venue. A booker should
immediately see professionalism and consistency when they
review your materials.

After you send your initial email, wait a week or two before
following up, and keep the reminder brief and courteous
with links to your materials. Persistence paired with
preparation shows that you are serious about the gig.

DON'T: Send Blanket Emails
Never blast the same generic message to every venue on your
list. A one-size-fits-all message signals that you have not
done your homework. Even in the early research stage, tailor
your outreach to reflect that you understand the venue's style
and audience.

DON'T: Overpromise
Do not claim you can draw a crowd of 200 if you cannot. Do
not say you have a polished three-hour set if you only have
90 minutes prepared. Bookers will remember false promises
long after they forget the music.

DON'T: Ignore Booking Instructions
If a venue asks for links in a certain format, a minimum
draw, or specific materials, provide them exactly as
requested. Professionals respect the process. Amateurs try to
shortcut it and pay the price.

DON'T: Ignore the Details in Your EPK
Spelling errors, broken links, or missing contact information
signal carelessness. A single oversight can cost you a
booking.

DON'T: Submit Amateur-Quality Media
Low-resolution photos, distorted audio, or poorly lit video clips make even great music look second-rate. If your materials don't meet the standard, wait until they do. First impressions are permanent.

DON'T: Let Your Digital Presence Go Stale
An outdated website, missing links, or inactive social profiles raise doubts before a booker even listens to your music. Keep everything current so your professionalism is clear at a glance.

DON'T: Underestimate Your Own Brand
If your photos, logo, or messaging feel inconsistent, a booker will question whether you can deliver a consistent show. Every piece of your presentation should tell the same story.

DON'T: Be Caught Off Guard About Your Fee
Know your numbers before you pitch. If you are new, research what comparable artists in your market are charging and set a realistic range. Your rates can grow with experience, but professionalism begins with being prepared now.

DON'T: Mistake Gigs for Practice
Playing often is not the same as practicing. A live performance is where you deliver, not where you prepare. Musicians who confuse the two eventually expose their weaknesses to the very audiences they are trying to win over.

Chapter 2: Approaching Venues

Aspiring Pro Mindset: Choose the Right Stage, Not Just Any Stage

A gigging musician will play anywhere. A professional musician seeks the stage that fits their brand, audience, and long-term goals. Not every venue is a good match. A packed room means nothing if the audience is not engaged, or if the space does not reflect the type of artist you are building yourself to be.

The professional understands that visibility without alignment is a waste of effort. They do not just want to play. They want to connect. They do not just want to be seen. They want to be remembered.

This is why research matters. Know the type of music the venue books. Learn the kind of audience they attract. Pay attention to how artists are promoted and whether your sound belongs in that environment. Before you send a single email, ask yourself:

- Will my target audience be here, or is this the audience I want to reach?

- Does this stage reflect the type of artist I am becoming?

- Will this performance propel me forward or divert me from my direction?

Chasing every opportunity will keep you busy. Chasing the right ones will build a career.

DO: Research Each Venue

Before you reach out, know who you are approaching. Study their schedule. Listen to the artists they book. Learn whether they lean toward original music, covers, or themed experiences. This preparation shows respect for the booker's time and demonstrates that you belong on their stage.

DO: Keep Your Message Concise

Bookers do not have time to read your life story. Your email should be brief and clear. Introduce yourself, describe what you offer, and provide links to your EPK or performance videos. Always close with a professional request for consideration. Short and polished beats long and scattered.

DO: Present Yourself as a Professional

Include links to high-quality videos. Avoid grainy, shaky, or poorly lit clips. Use a professional email address. Make sure your social media reflects the same level of polish you want the venue to see. Consistency matters.

DO: Know Your Worth

As noted in Chapter 1, have your numbers ready before you pitch. When asked about your fee, answer with clarity and confidence.

If a venue offers less than your minimum, respond respectfully and explain what your standard rate includes. You can also explore adjustments such as shortening the set, reducing the band size, or restructuring the performance to fit the budget.

DO: Follow Up With Professionalism

Persistence matters. If you do not hear back, wait a week or two and send a short, polite follow-up. Respect the process. The right balance is being present without being pushy.

DON'T: Disrespect the Process
Every venue has its way of doing things. If the instructions say to submit through a form, use it. If they ask for EPK links, do not send your Instagram. Skipping steps does not make you clever. It makes you careless.

DON'T: Act Entitled
Even if you have shared stages with well-known names, remember that every new venue is an audition. Humility earns more respect than boasting. Confidence is good, but entitlement will close doors.

DON'T: Oversell Yourself
Do not claim you have opened for an artist if you were simply on the same festival lineup. Do not inflate your draw if you cannot back it up. Exaggeration will catch up with you. Bookers talk, and your reputation follows you.

DON'T: Ignore Money Conversations
Avoiding the fee discussion or saying "whatever you can pay me" weakens your position. Be clear, be realistic, and be confident. If you do not establish your worth, others will decide it for you, and rarely in your favor.

Approaching a venue is more than sending an email. It is presenting yourself as a professional, aligning with the right stages, and handling the money conversation with clarity and respect.

Chapter 3: Negotiation Essentials

Aspiring Pro Mindset: Value First, Price Second

Many musicians avoid conversations about money, afraid of losing the gig or being seen as difficult. Professionals know that money is part of the music business. Talking about fees does not make you greedy. It makes you prepared.

Negotiation is not about winning or losing. It is about finding fair terms that respect both the artist and the venue. Professionals frame their fees around value, which includes the experience they deliver, the audience they attract, and the professionalism they bring, rather than simply naming a number.

When you negotiate with clarity and confidence, you protect your art, your time, and your reputation.

DO: Research Market Rates
Know what artists at your level are charging in your area. Rates vary by city, venue type, and genre. If you are new, start with realistic numbers that reflect your experience while aiming for steady growth. Being informed allows you to negotiate from a position of knowledge, not guesswork.

DO: Present Your Fee with Confidence
As emphasized in the previous chapters, your numbers should already be set. In negotiation, the focus is on how you communicate them. Rather than simply stating a figure, frame your fee as a package of value. For example, explain that your rate covers preparation, travel, and equipment. This helps the booker understand what they are paying for and shows professionalism beyond the performance itself.

DO: Offer Scaled Options
Flexibility shows professionalism. Instead of discounting immediately, offer scaled choices. A solo performance might cost one amount, a duo another, and a full band a higher fee. This allows venues to choose what fits their budget while keeping your value intact.

DO: Ask for Deposits When Appropriate
For gigs that require travel, significant preparation, or block out high-demand dates, consider asking for a deposit. Deposits confirm commitment and protect you if the event is cancelled. Standard deposits range from 25 to 50 percent of the total fee. However, keep in mind that smaller venues often do not provide deposits due to limited operating capital, so do not assume they are always part of the deal. Always be flexible.

DO: Put It in Writing
Every agreement, including negotiated terms, must be in writing. Confirm changes in an updated contract or email. Clear documentation prevents misunderstandings and ensures accountability.

DON'T: Accept "Exposure" as Payment
Exposure does not pay bills. Unless the event offers unique, high-value visibility that can be leveraged into paid work, exposure is rarely worth your time. Professionals know when to decline politely and save their energy for opportunities that respect their craft.

DON'T: Undersell Yourself Out of Fear
Do not say yes to every lowball offer just to stay busy. Consistently accepting less teaches bookers that you will always work for less. Protect your floor. Once you establish it, stand by it.

DON'T: Negotiate Emotionally
Keep your emotions in check. If the venue cannot meet your fee, thank them and move on. Professionals do not argue, complain, or pressure. They negotiate respectfully and know when to walk away.

DON'T: Forget the Power of Silence
Sometimes the strongest part of a negotiation is what you do not say. After you state your fee, wait. Let the booker respond. Filling silence with discounts or justifications weakens your position. Professionals know how to state their value and let it stand.

Negotiation is not a battle. It is a professional conversation about value, respect, and fairness. When you know your worth, present it with confidence, and protect it in writing, you set the tone for a career built on respect and sustainability.

Chapter 4: The Power of the Contract

Aspiring Pro Mindset: Secure It In Writing

A gigging musician shows up and hopes for the best. An aspiring professional secures the agreement in writing before a single note is played. Handshakes, texts, and verbal promises may feel convenient, but they are also the fastest way for things to go wrong. Professionals protect their name, their time, and their money with contracts.

A contract is more than paperwork. It is communication in writing. It clarifies responsibilities, confirms expectations, and protects both you and the venue. When an agreement is clear, there is no confusion, no "I thought," and no relying on memory weeks later. It signals to the venue that you are not just a performer but a professional doing business.

DO: Use a Contract Every Time
Even if the venue provides a contract, review it carefully and ask questions. If the venue does not provide one, send your own. At minimum, confirm the details in an email that both sides agree to. Written confirmation protects your credibility and eliminates misunderstandings.

A professional performance contract should include:

- **Performance details**: Date, load-in time, soundcheck, start and end time, and breakdown.

- **Compensation**: Fee, deposit if required, and deadline for final payment.

- **Cancellation policy**: What happens if the venue cancels and what happens if you do.

- **Technical needs**: What the venue provides and what you are expected to bring.

- **Behavior expectations**: Venue rules about attire, alcohol, or conduct on stage.

- **Guest or sit-in policy**: Who is allowed to join you on stage or backstage.

DO: Negotiate with Flexibility and Confidence

Not every stage has the same budget. A small lounge will not pay the same as a corporate event or festival. Flexibility does not mean devaluing yourself. It means knowing how to scale.

Be prepared to offer different options. For example, quote one rate for a solo set, a higher rate for a duo, and another for a full band. This gives the booker choices without forcing you to undersell your worth.

Ask for a deposit when appropriate, especially if travel or significant preparation is required. Deposits protect against last-minute cancellations and show that the venue is committed.

If a venue's budget is below your standard fee, you can adjust respectfully by trimming the set length, reducing the ensemble size, or discussing other forms of value such as promotion, media coverage, or merchandise opportunities. Always frame your fee around the value you bring, not just the time you spend on stage.

DO: Clarify Payment Terms Upfront
Never assume. State clearly how and when you expect to be paid, whether by check, cash, or digital transfer. Confirm whether payment happens before the show begins, during intermission, or at the end of the night.

A professional also clarifies who will be issuing payment. Is it the venue owner, the manager, or the event organizer They may not be the same person, and knowing this prevents last-minute confusion.

DO: Recognize the Red Flags
Be cautious of:

- Vague language such as "as discussed" without specific details.

- Verbal promises that are not written into the agreement.

- No cancellation or rescheduling policy.

- Unclear or delayed payment terms.

- Offers of "exposure" instead of pay.

When you see red flags, ask for changes or walk away. Protecting your professionalism is more valuable than taking a questionable gig.

DON'T: Sign Without Reading

Do not skim the agreement. Read every line. If you do not understand a clause, ask. If something feels unfair, request a revision. Signing blindly leaves you vulnerable to unpleasant surprises later.

DON'T: Work Without Written Confirmation

Never accept "We'll take care of you" or "You'll be fine" as payment terms. If it is not written down, it does not exist. Professionals put it in writing. Amateurs rely on memory and regret it later.

DON'T: Ignore Deposits

If the gig requires travel, significant rehearsal, or holds a prime date that prevents you from booking other work, ask for a deposit. Skipping this step leaves you exposed if the show is cancelled at the last minute.

DON'T: Undervalue Yourself

Do not let fear of losing a gig push you into agreeing to less than your minimum value. Saying yes to every low offer teaches bookers that you are willing to work for less. Professionals negotiate respectfully, but they know their floor and they hold it.

Contracts turn conversations into commitments. They protect your time, your money, and your reputation. A professional never leaves the details to chance.

Chapter 5: Respect the House System

Aspiring Pro Mindset: Work With the Sound, Not Against It

A common mistake some musicians make is to assume consistency across venues. They believe that what worked or was allowed at one gig is automatically acceptable at the next. For example, they may show up with excessive speakers and unnecessary gear without prior permission.

Every room is different, and professionalism means knowing what is truly needed for the gig, communicating with the venue owner in advance, and respecting the space, the system in place, and the people running it.

If you cannot hear yourself properly during a performance, the issue is likely not the house system. In most cases, it is the stage volume due to other musicians playing too loudly. Adding extra gear only clutters the stage, turns music into noise, and diminishes the overall guest experience.

DO: Communicate With the Venue Owner
Determine what is needed for the gig ahead of time. This ensures you arrive prepared, avoid unnecessary surprises, and maintain a professional relationship with the venue.

DO: Communicate With the Engineer
Use soundcheck to work through issues. A professional communicates clearly with the sound crew and adjusts as needed. The engineer wants you to sound your best, but they cannot help if you bypass the system. Working with them ensures the audience hears music, not noise.

DO: Control Your Stage Volume

Remember that louder is not better. Balance on stage is what allows the sound engineer to create a clean mix for the audience. Keep your volume in check so everyone can hear and play their part.

DON'T: Bring Unnecessary Gear

Respect the venue's investment in its sound. Bringing your own gear when a system is already in place disrupts the flow of the night, undermines the engineer, and adds unnecessary noise. If you cannot hear properly, ask for a monitor adjustment instead of adding speakers.

DON'T: Assume Every Venue Is the Same

What was allowed or worked at one gig may not be acceptable at the next. Each venue has its own expectations, systems, and space. Arriving with assumptions makes you look unprofessional. Treat every gig as unique, and show the venue you respect their standards.

Chapter 6: Maximize the Performance

Aspiring Pro Mindset: Deliver the Full Experience

A gigging musician shows up to play songs. A professional delivers an experience. Music is at the center, but what audiences and venues remember is the energy, the presence, and the way you made them feel. Professionals understand that the performance is not just about the setlist. It is about creating a moment worth remembering.

This chapter is about mastering the art of performance, building connection with the audience, and showing venues that you bring value beyond the music.

DO: Bring Energy and Presence
Audiences respond to more than sound. They respond to confidence, body language, and how you carry yourself. Make eye contact, move with the rhythm, and project energy that fills the room. A strong presence can elevate even the simplest song.

DO: Connect with the Audience
A performance is a conversation, not a recital. Talk to your audience. Share an occasional brief story between songs. Acknowledge the people in the room. Connection builds loyalty, and loyalty brings them back not just for the music, but for you.

DO: Support the Venue's Atmosphere

Every venue has its own vibe. A supper club requires a different tone than a festival stage. Pay attention to the space and the crowd. Professionals know how to adapt without compromising their style. Aligning with the venue makes you memorable and respected.

DO: Add Value Beyond the Stage

Think about how you can contribute to the success of the night beyond playing. Encourage the audience to support the venue by ordering food or drinks. A simple acknowledgment of the staff goes a long way. Venues notice the artists who help create a positive experience for everyone.

DO: Pace Your Set with Intention

Plan your setlist as a journey. Start with energy, build momentum, create peaks, and give space for quieter moments. A well-paced performance feels like a story unfolding, not just a list of songs.

DON'T: Treat Every Song the Same

Variety keeps audiences engaged. Mix tempos, moods, and dynamics. Audiences notice when the same songs show up in the same order every time. Keep things fresh by rotating tunes, surprising your crowd with new material, or reworking familiar songs. A refreshed setlist shows growth, keeps your following engaged, and gives people a reason to return.

DON'T: Overindulge in Stage Banter

Talking too much between songs can lose the audience. Keep stories short and relevant. Share just enough to create connection without slowing the momentum of the show.

DON'T: Turn the Stage into a Soapbox
Your views are your own. The audience came for music, not a diatribe or a sermon. Political commentary and religious messages can divide a room and shift the focus away from the experience you are paid to deliver.

Consider the venue neutral ground where guests of all backgrounds can relax without being pulled into personal beliefs. Unless a venue specifically books you for a themed event, keep those views off the mic. Professionalism means leaving the spotlight on the music and giving every guest a night they can enjoy without distraction.

DON'T: Air Your Laundry on Stage
If you are having issues with your band or a band member, the stage is not the place to address it. Audiences should never witness arguments, side comments, or tension between musicians. It distracts from the performance, damages your image, and makes the venue regret trusting you with their stage.

Professionalism means handling conflicts privately. Whatever disagreements exist, put them aside until after the show. The audience came for music, not a front-row seat to your problems.

DON'T: Disrespect the Audience
Audiences know when you are going through the motions. They also know when you are distracted, unprepared, or treating the show like a rehearsal. Professionals give their best effort whether there are ten people in the room or a hundred.

DON'T: Forget Who Is Watching
The audience includes more than paying guests. The staff, the manager, and potential future bookers may be in the room. A careless comment or sloppy performance can travel further than you think.

A performance is not just about playing music. It is about creating a memorable experience that connects with the audience and adds value to the venue. Professionals leave both the crowd and the booker wanting more.

Chapter 7: Playing to the Room

Aspiring Pro Mindset: Understanding Balance and Respect for the ears

One of the most overlooked aspects of performance is not the notes, but the sound itself. An aspiring professional knows that playing to the room is just as important as playing the music. Volume, tone, and balance are not afterthoughts. They are part of your instrument. Respecting the ears of your audience, your bandmates, and the venue is a mark of maturity. Professionals adapt their sound to the space they are in, knowing that the goal is not to overpower, but to connect.

How you play to the room matters just as much as what you play. Musicians often forget that they are not only on stage to perform. They are also part of a larger experience. Guests purchase tickets to enjoy a curated evening. The staff is working to maintain a certain atmosphere. The venue has invested in acoustics and sound to create a specific kind of experience. When your sound overwhelms that, you diminish the very thing you were hired to uphold.

The Role of Volume

Volume is not power. Too loud and your sound becomes noise. Too soft and your performance fades into the background. The mark of a professional is knowing how to adjust and allowing dynamics to carry emotion rather than sheer loudness.

Too often, high volume is a common issue in intimate venues. Drummers who pound the drums and cymbals as if they are playing in an arena. Guitarists who perform like Jimi Hendrix or Prince at a heightened volume. Singers who scream because their band is drowning them out. Horn players who overpower the room and leave guests complaining about the excessive loudness of the music.

These musicians treat every venue the same. They take a one size fits all approach and mistake the intimate setting of small space for a nightclub or festival.

Balance Within the Band
No instrument should dominate the entire show. Balance is what makes music breathe. Listening to each other on stage is just as important as playing your part. When the band adjusts as a unit, the audience feels the harmony in more ways than one.

Respect for the Space
Every room has its own character. A lounge is not a stadium. A dinner show is not a festival stage. Professionals adapt. They recognize that sound in a small, intimate space must be controlled, that acoustics change depending on layout and crowd size.

They also understand that audiences are different. What feels energetic and exciting for a younger crowd can feel overwhelming for a more mature audience. Playing too loud for a dinner show or older guests will not keep them engaged, it will drive them away.

Professionals pay attention to the room, adjusting volume and delivery so the experience fits the space as well as the audience. Musicians who treat every stage as the same show quickly lose opportunities.

Follow Direction

When a sound engineer, venue owner, or bandleader asks you to adjust, it is not a critique of your talent. It is about protecting the guest experience. Those who take that feedback and adjust earn respect. Those who resist it often don't return.

DO

- Pay attention to how your sound fills the space.

- Work with your bandmates to maintain balance.

- Recognize that every venue has its own acoustics and adapt accordingly.

- Welcome feedback from the sound engineer, staff, or venue owner as part of professionalism.

DON'T

- Equate volume with impact. Loudness is not the same as power.

- Ignore the audience's body language. If they're wincing or leaning away, you're too loud.

- Play as though you're in an arena when you're in an intimate lounge.

- Argue with or dismiss those tasked with protecting the guest experience.

Musicians who adapt to the space earn the return, because they give audiences what they came for: an experience that feels right.

Chapter 8: Dos and Don'ts at the Venue

Aspiring Pro Mindset: Treat Every Stage Like the Big Stage

Professionals approach every room with the same level of respect and preparation, whether it holds fifty people or five hundred. They do not wait for a major break to act like professionals. They understand that every performance is an audition for the next one, every interaction is part of their reputation, and every guest deserves a first-class experience.

The way you treat the venue, the staff, and the stage speaks just as loudly as the way you perform. Professionals show up ready, respectful, and intentional. Amateurs cut corners and reveal themselves in small ways that cost them future bookings.

DO: Arrive Early
Arriving with time to spare shows respect for the venue's schedule. It gives you time to set up without rushing, to check in with staff, and to settle into the space. Musicians who arrive early communicate professionalism before they ever play a note.

DO: Use Soundcheck Wisely
Soundcheck is not rehearsal. It is about balance, clarity, and readiness. Come prepared so you can make quick adjustments. Treat the process with respect for the engineer's role and the venue's time.

DO: Communicate Clearly with Staff
Introduce yourself to the sound engineer, manager, and anyone involved in the production of the show. Confirm set times, breaks, and any specific expectations. Clear communication prevents confusion later.

DO: Promote the Venue
When you tag the venue, thank them publicly, or mention them on stage, you strengthen the partnership. Venues remember the artists who support them, not just the ones who play there.

DO: Keep Your Setup Tidy
A cluttered stage looks careless. Keep cables, cases, and personal items organized. Respect the space as if another artist will be walking in after you — because one probably will.

DO: Handle Tabs and Gratuities with Respect
If you order food or drinks, settle your bill promptly and tip your server fairly. Never assume your fee covers your tab unless it is clearly stated in your contract, and never put the staff in a position where they must chase you for payment. The way you handle money with the team is a direct reflection of your professionalism.

DON'T: Overstay Your Set Time
Respect the show schedule. Even if the crowd is loving it, running long can disrupt guests, the venue or staff and may create overtime costs. Ending on time leaves a stronger impression and often makes audiences eager to return for your next show.

DON'T: Touch the Venue's Equipment Without Permission
Do not adjust, unplug, or move equipment without asking. Boundaries matter. Professionals respect the venue's gear and the people responsible for it.

DON'T: Disrespect Staff
Every person working at the venue contributes to the success of your performance. From the server to the sound engineer, their opinions matter. Rudeness or dismissiveness will travel quickly and can cost you future opportunities.

DON'T: Discuss Your Fee in Front of Staff or Guests
Money conversations should be handled privately and professionally. Talking about your rate in the room makes you appear unprofessional and can create tension with staff. Handle financial matters discreetly with the booker or manager.

DON'T: Leave a Mess Behind
When you leave the stage or green room, it should be as clean as you found it. Wrappers, cups, tangled cables, or forgotten gear signal carelessness. Respect the space so you are remembered as easy to work with, not as a burden to clean up after.

DON'T: Expect Complimentary Seats
Some musicians show up with children, significant others, or friends and expect the venue to provide complimentary seats. Unless this has been discussed and approved in advance, that expectation is unprofessional.

Every seat in a venue represents potential revenue. When you take one without permission, you are asking the venue to lose money on your behalf.

Think of it this way: you would not bring your child, friends, or significant other to your day job or workplace and expect them to be accommodated. A paid booking is no different. It should be treated with the same professionalism you would bring to any other job.

Professionals clarify guest arrangements before the gig. If you want someone on your list, ask ahead of time and respect the answer.

Venues notice who treats their space like a business and who treats it like a personal hangout. One earns respect, the other costs you future bookings.

Chapter 9: Mistakes That Will Cost You

Aspiring Pro Mindset: Earn the return

The fastest way to earn bookings is to act like a professional. The fastest way to lose them is through careless mistakes. Venues talk, staff talk, and word travels quickly. Protect your career by avoiding these mistakes at all costs.

Showing Up Late
If you are late to soundcheck or to the stage, you are already telling the venue that you can't be trusted. Reliability is part of professionalism.

Overpromising and Underdelivering
Saying you can draw a crowd, play for hours, or handle a certain setup when you can't will end your relationship with a venue before it begins.

Playing Too Loud
Volume without control drives audiences away. Literally. If multiple guests are leaving mid-show, you are likely missing the mark. If guests are wincing or complaining, your music is not connecting. Every venue is different. Professionals know how to adjust to the room rather than overpower it.

Disrespecting Staff
Servers, bartenders, and sound engineers have influence. If you are rude or dismissive, your name will move to the bottom of the booking list or be deleted altogether.

Bringing Unapproved Guests
Bringing unapproved guests, as noted in Chapter 8, is unprofessional and can cost you future bookings.

Avoiding the Money Conversation
Saying "whatever you can pay me" or avoiding your fee signals that you do not know your worth. Venues expect clarity. Without it, you will always be undervalued.

Complaining Publicly
Talking negatively about the venue on social media or to other musicians damages your reputation far more than it damages theirs. Word spreads, and professionalism is questioned.

Leaving a Mess
Walking away from the stage or green room without cleaning up signals carelessness. Venues remember the burden, not the music.

Using the Stage as Your Rehearsal Space
One of the fastest ways to lose future bookings is to treat a live show as your practice session. Venues are not paying you to figure out your set on stage. Audiences did not buy tickets to watch you rehearse. When your songs are half-prepared or your band is still working out transitions in front of paying guests, it tells the venue that you are not ready and that you do not respect their room.

If you are serious about your career, you will never use a show as a substitute for preparation.

Being Impaired
Nothing undermines your professionalism faster than arriving to a gig visibly under the influence. It affects your performance, your reliability, and your reputation. Venues and audiences expect you to bring your best self, not a compromised version.

Chapter 10: After the Gig

Aspiring Pro Mindset: The Show Isn't Over When the Music Ends

Many musicians think the job is done once the last note fades. Professionals know the performance continues after the gig. The way you handle follow-up, payment, and communication determines whether the venue sees you as a one-time act or a trusted partner worth bringing back.

Closing the night with professionalism sets the stage for the next opportunity.

DO: Handle Payment Professionally
Confirm payment before the night begins so there are no surprises. After the show, collect your payment respectfully and discreetly. If you are invoicing, send the invoice promptly with clear details of the performance, agreed-upon fee, and payment due date.

Keep records of every payment you receive. This not only protects you but also helps you build a history of rates that you can use to negotiate higher fees in the future.

DO: Thank the Venue and Staff
Gratitude goes a long way. Thank the booker, manager, sound engineer, and staff before you leave. Acknowledging their role in the success of the night creates goodwill and makes you memorable for the right reasons.

DO: Review the Experience
After the gig, take time to reflect. What went well? What could improve? Did the setlist flow? Did the crowd respond the way you hoped? Self-assessment is how professionals grow.

DO: Follow Up With the Venue
Within a few days, send a short note thanking the venue for the opportunity. If you want to play there again, say so directly. Share photos, video clips, or positive audience feedback if available. Venues are more likely to rebook artists who stay engaged after the show.

Failing to follow up makes it harder for the venue to remember you when planning future shows.

DO: Leverage the Performance
Post highlights on your website and social media. Tag the venue and acknowledge the audience. Sharing your performance builds your brand, supports the venue, and gives potential bookers proof of your professionalism and crowd connection.

DO: Respect the Load-Out Process
Break down your equipment quickly and efficiently. Venues often have tight schedules, and lingering on stage or blocking staff while they reset the room creates frustration. Pack up neatly and move your gear out of the way as soon as possible.

DO: Acknowledge Your Audience
If fans approach you after the show, give them a moment. A quick thank-you, a handshake, or a photo can turn a one-time listener into a loyal supporter. Audience connection after the show matters just as much as during it.

DON'T: Forget to Promote Future Engagements
If you have another performance scheduled at the same venue, mention it in your follow-up or when posting highlights. Missing this opportunity means missing a chance to build momentum with the audience and the venue.

DON'T: Delay Invoicing
Waiting weeks to send an invoice signals disorganization. Bookers and managers work with many artists. If your paperwork is late, payment will be too.

DON'T: Overstay Your Welcome
Do not linger for hours after your set, especially if the venue needs to close or reset. Socializing has its place, but professionals know when it is time to leave.

DON'T: Bad-mouth the Venue
Even if something went wrong, never vent about it publicly. Word travels quickly in the music community. Professionals address issues privately and respectfully. Complaining on social media damages your reputation more than it damages the venue.

DON'T: Forget to Archive Contracts and Receipts
Keep copies of every agreement and proof of payment. These records protect you in case of disputes and simplify your finances at tax time. Treat your music career like the business it is.

What you do after the music ends is often what people remember most.

Chapter 11: The Stories Behind the Standards

Every standard in this book was born from lived experience. These are not rules written in theory. They are the result of nights on the stage, moments with musicians, and lessons learned the hard way. Some came from artists who stumbled, others from artists who continue to shine. Together, these stories explain why the standards exist and what they mean in practice.

The Musician Who Stood Me Up

Guitarist Jmichael Peeples has been one of my go-to musicians since before the doors of Chayz Lounge opened. Reliable and professional, he has come through for me more than once, but in this particular incident he didn't just come through for me. He saved the show, my brand, and my reputation, and it is a moment I will never forget.

I was preparing for the grand opening of Chayz Lounge. The band was booked, the contract signed, the finishing touches were being put on the space, the show was sold out, and excitement was building. Just a week before the big night, the manager for the artist scheduled to perform called to inform me that his artist would no longer appear because he had accepted a gig opening for Sinbad. The manager tried to justify it as an opportunity his artist couldn't turn down, but there was no persuading him to honor the contract.

My first call was to Jmichael. I explained the dilemma. He told me to give him a few hours and said he'd see what he could pull together.

Later that evening, he called back with the news that not only could he fill the spot for the grand opening, but he had also reached out to national recording artist Paula Atherton, who agreed to join him. Jmichael not only saved me in a pinch and protected my brand, but together he and Paula delivered a stellar performance.

To this day, eight years later, many of the guests who attended still recall that evening of June 4, 2017 as the best time they ever had.

Fast forward to 2023. After a show, a member of the backing band of the evening's headliner approached me with excitement. He said he had a friend who wanted to perform at my venue and would be a perfect fit. He had the musician on speakerphone, and the artist on the other end was equally enthusiastic. When I heard the name, I couldn't believe it. It was the same musician who had stood me up for my grand opening. I reminded him of that incident and explained why he would never grace my stage. He stuttered, at a loss for words. The musician who brought the phone to me was stunned as well, admitting he had no idea that had ever happened.

Opportunities come with responsibility. When you abandon your commitments, you not only lose the gig, you lose trust. And trust, once broken, rarely returns. Venue owners, booking agents, and decision-makers may remember the good musicians, but more often it is the unprofessional ones who remain etched in their memory. Keep in mind, they talk. Make sure your name is mentioned in a good way.

The Artist Who Showed Up Late

The show was scheduled for 8:00 PM. Our doors opened at 6:30, and by 7:30 every guest was seated. Many had already ordered food, drinks were flowing, and the energy in the room was full of anticipation. I am known for starting shows on time, whether or not every guest has arrived. So at 8:00, eyes shifted toward the stage with expectation. Plates ceased to clink, conversations quieted. The stage sat empty.

The artist walked in at 8:10, dragging equipment, rushing to set up, muttering apologies under his breath. In his haste, he bent to plug in a cable and revealed more than the guests cared to see, yet he never stopped to correct himself. The moment only deepened the sense of disorder. The audience's excitement soured. Instead of enjoying a seamless start to their evening, guests were watching chaos unfold. There was no soundcheck, the monitors were never balanced, and the performance stumbled from the first note and never recovered. The audience disconnected. Instead of listening, chatter filled the room.

What the artist failed to see is that lateness is not just about time. It is about trust. The guests trusted the show to start as promised. The staff trusted the flow of the evening. I trusted him to uphold the standard of excellence and the terms of the contract he signed. In ten minutes, that trust was broken.

He was not invited back. Not because of the music, but because of the message his behavior sent. It said, "My time is more valuable than yours." *That message cost him more than one show. It cost him his reputation in the room.*

The Singer Who Overpromised

The call came with enthusiasm. The musician assured me he had a polished show, appropriate material for a two-hour set, and a strong following that would fill my room. His confidence was persuasive. On top of that, he boasted about being a Billboard chart-topping artist. On paper, it sounded like a win for everyone — my guests, my staff, and the artist. Skipping my usual vetting process, I trusted his word and booked the show.

The night arrived. Guests filled their tables, expecting an evening of music and energy. The singer began strong, but by 8:45 the cracks showed. Songs were repeated, transitions stalled, and the once-confident performance lost its shine. The band did their best to pick up the slack, but it was not enough. It was clear the musician was ill prepared.

The promised "strong following" also never materialized. The room was not empty, but it was far from the turnout I had been led to expect. Many of the guests were repeat customers, and the new guests who came for the advertised experience were disappointed. By 9:00, some began to leave. Along with them went the chance for the artist to win over what could have been a new and loyal fanbase.

Overpromising may secure a booking once, but it will not secure the next. The disappointment fell not only on the artist, but on me for trusting what was said. I hold my stage to a standard, and I expect those who stand on it to honor their commitments. This singer did not.

Promises are not just words. In this business, they are commitments. And commitments, once broken, close doors.

The Musician Who Disrespected the Staff

It was a busy night. The room was full, the energy was right, and my staff was working hard to make sure guests were cared for. The artist, however, seemed determined to make the evening more difficult than it needed to be.

From the start, he treated the servers as if they were his personal servants. He made unreasonable demands about his orders and even snapped his fingers at one instead of calling her by name. The tension was felt by everyone around him. When he was on stage, he referred to the bartender as "hey" and told her to make him another drink. At that point, I had to decide whether to air dirty laundry in front of guests or deal with it another way. I chose the latter. Picking up the extra mic, I said jokingly, "Your private bartender is tied up at the moment." Guests laughed, and he got the message.

What he failed to realize is that the staff is the backbone of the experience. They create the atmosphere our guests expect and the environment that allows the artist to shine. When you disrespect them, you disrespect the entire venue. Guests may not always hear the words exchanged backstage or see the gestures, but they can feel the energy when a performer carries arrogance into the room. That night, the atmosphere shifted.

After the show, my staff made their feelings clear. They did not want him back. I needed no convincing. I had already come to the same conclusion. I rely on my team. They work hard to maintain the standard my venue is known for, and any artist who undermines them undermines me.

Talent alone is never enough. No matter how gifted you are, if you cannot treat people with respect, your opportunities will shrink. That musician played his last show on my stage the night he disrespected the very people who supported him.

Respect for staff is not optional. It is the foundation of professionalism.

The Saxophonist Who Saved the Night

Not every story is about mistakes. Some artists stand out for the right reasons, and they remind me why I opened my doors in the first place.

Before Chayz Lounge, I was producing shows at various venues around the city. One in particular seated about 150 people, and on this night, the headliner was a notable musician. Every seat was filled, the anticipation was high, and the stage was set for an unforgettable evening.

The headliner was scheduled to arrive 90 minutes before showtime. I had worked with him twice before and knew his setup was simple, so I wasn't overly concerned about a long soundcheck. But as the clock ticked closer to 7:00 PM, there was still no sign of him. Calls went unanswered.

Thankfully, I had booked an opening act, Jon Stot "Juru" Jones, a smooth jazz saxophonist, to play a 45-minute set. The show began on time, as it always does, and Jon took the stage. My hope was that the headliner would walk through the door before Jon wrapped. He did not.

Jon kept going. At 8:30, still no headliner. By then, Jon had not only played well beyond his set, but he had also engaged and entertained the audience with energy and charm. At 9:15, despite my updates to the crowd that the headliner was en route, some guests were understandably restless. Jon never flinched. He continued to give the audience a show.

Finally, at 9:30, the headliner arrived. To his credit, he gave a performance that made the audience feel the wait had been worth it. But the real credit of the night went to Jon.

His professionalism and willingness to carry the weight of the evening saved more than just the show. He saved my reputation at a time when I was still building my brand and audience.

That night reminded me of something deeper: ***true professionals do not just play their set. They rise to the moment. Jon did that, and it made all the difference.***

The Singer Who Forgot the Standards

There was once a singer who was a fixture on my stage for years, a dependable draw and one of my go-to acts. Her voice was wonderful, her stage presence magnetic, and her song knowledge extensive, yet she aligned with a band that lacked experience and carried a limited repertoire. Despite repeated conversations, the group rarely rehearsed for their ticketed shows and relied on the same set list. As the lead, she failed to address the matter responsibly.

The issue came to a head during a two-night ticketed engagement that was heavily promoted as two completely different shows, with separate flyer designs making the promise clear to everyone. Guests who purchased tickets for both nights expected a fresh experience, but each performance mirrored their previous free shows and the two ticketed sets were virtually identical. No apology was offered, only excuses about a last-minute personnel change that did not hold up under scrutiny.

That weekend became their final appearance at Chayz Lounge, a reminder that preparation, professionalism, and respect for the audience, especially a paying audience, are not suggestions. They are the standard.

A strong voice or loyal following cannot cover for a lack of rehearsal or respect for the audience. A true professional treats every show as unique, rehearses accordingly, and leaves the audience eager for the next performance, not questioning their ticket purchase.

The Band That Trashed the Space

Our room was well-dressed and ready. Tables and chairs were sanitized and set, candles were lit, and every detail was polished for the evening ahead. The stage was waiting, the atmosphere set. Then the band arrived.

Instead of heading straight to the stage, they dropped gear cases onto guest tables and scattered equipment across the room. One musician set his drink on a table that had already been cleaned and dressed. Another opened a food container and started eating in a corner reserved for patrons. Altogether, they occupied six tables. In an instant, the polished room felt less like a venue for a show and more like a space being crashed by an uninvited group.

My staff had to clean the room once again. They wiped down tables, re-centered candles, and fixed what had just been finalized minutes earlier. Not one member of the band apologized for the disruption, for creating extra work, or for treating the space without care. They acted as if this was normal. And when the show ended, they left their trash behind in the very room they had occupied.

What they failed to realize is that the moment you walk into a venue, you are being observed. Staff notice. Management notices. Early guests notice. Respect the space as if it is already full of people, because soon it will be.

First impressions don't start on stage. They start the moment you walk through the door.

The Singer Who Crossed the Line

I first met her when she performed alongside another musician. Her voice was incredible, and I was impressed enough to book her for her own show. Everything leading up to that night went as it should. The contract was signed without issue, she shared a setlist that looked solid, and she arrived on time. Soundcheck was seamless, and all was well when she left to return to her hotel to change.

When she came back later, she seemed a bit hyper, almost overly excited, but I attributed it to pre-show jitters. Once the show began, what I thought were nerves quickly proved to be something else entirely.

Her antics on stage were provocative, beyond anything I or my guests expected. She flirted openly with male guests, some of whom were seated with their wives or girlfriends. At one point, she used one of the supporting columns in the room as if she were swinging around a pole. She spoke at length between songs, telling intimate and off-color stories. At one point, she even left the stage, wandered through the audience, and took a sip of someone's drink — uninvited. The behavior continued throughout her set.

During the break, I pulled her aside to address her actions. It was then I realized she was under the influence of some kind of substance. After much back-and-forth about her performance, I made the decision not to allow her back on stage. Instead, I let the band finish the evening on their own.

I apologized directly to the guests. Some were understanding, while others were frustrated. To those, I offered tickets to another show as a way to make up for the poor experience.

When all the guests were gone, she attempted to excuse her actions by saying she was just nervous. Then she asked a question I did not anticipate — if she could return for a do-over. When I calmly explained why that would not happen, she stormed out and told me off on the way. The next day, she blasted both me and Chayz Lounge on social media.

That night was a reminder that **professionalism is not just about showing up on time, signing contracts, or rehearsing a setlist. It is about showing respect for the audience, the venue, and yourself.**

She never returned to my stage.

The Violinist Who Hijacked the Stage

The headliner that night was a musician I'd worked with a few times before. Solid. Dependable. Professional. Always respectful of the venue and its staff. So when he mentioned bringing in a guest violinist to sit in for a few numbers, I agreed without hesitation. I didn't know her, but I trusted his judgment.

That trust was tested the moment the violinist walked in.

Without speaking to anyone, she headed straight for the stage and began pulling cables, unplugging equipment, shifting microphones, and rearranging the layout. The sound engineer looked at me as if to say, *Who is this?* Before I could even reach her, she had already overridden our setup.

When I asked her calmly to stop, she snapped. She told me I had no right to speak to her, then unleashed a stream of profanity that echoed louder than any instrument in the building. Needless to say, she never performed. But the real lesson wasn't hers. It was the headliner's. That moment nearly cost him his relationship with me and my venue.

He recognized how damaging the situation could have been and apologized profusely. It took time, but accountability opened the door to future opportunities.

The lesson here is simple... Anyone you bring with you represents you. If they act out, you're the one who pays the price.

The Musician Who Stepped Forward

Rodney Foster Jr., first came to my attention as part of the backing band for a singer who had performed at Chayz Lounge a few times. I didn't know much about him beyond the fact that he was always on time, always prepared, played well, and clearly took his craft seriously. For two years, he remained consistent in those qualities.

Then came the test. A nationally known musician cancelled just one week before his scheduled show. I reached out to Rodney, explained the situation, and asked if he would be willing to step up. He questioned whether he could carry a two-hour show on his own since he was accustomed to being in the background. But I had confidence in him. That night, he delivered an outstanding performance that the audience thoroughly enjoyed. It was the birth of Rod Foster & Company.

Shortly after, Covid forced the world to shut down. When it was time to reopen, I reached out to Rodney again. He put together a trio that became our Thursday night band, sometimes playing to only a handful of people. His professionalism, consistency, and dedication to his craft never wavered. In time, those qualities led me to ask him to become the leader of the Chayz Lounge House Band. Eight years later, Rod Foster & Company still have a home at Chayz Lounge, holding their space on my stage.

Reliability and consistency may not always get applause, but they earn trust. And when the spotlight finds you, even unexpectedly, that trust becomes the opportunity to rise as a true professional.

The Band That Brought the Bar

A band scheduled to perform arrived early and was placed in a private space to relax before their set. Instead of settling in quietly, they pulled out bottles of liquor and solo cups and began drinking. What should have been a moment of preparation turned into a scene that looked more like a tailgate party than a professional performance.

It was careless, and worse, it put my liquor license at risk. At my venue, every drink is accounted for, and every pour must follow strict guidelines. Allowing outside alcohol is not just against policy. It is against the law. If a guest or inspector had seen it, the consequences could have been devastating for my business.

What that band failed to understand is that professionalism extends beyond the stage. The way you carry yourself behind closed doors matters just as much as how you perform in front of an audience. For me, their choice raised a clear red flag: if they could not respect something as basic and serious as liquor laws, what else would they disregard?

They never played my stage again.

Respecting the room means respecting the space, the staff, the guests, and the business itself. Anything less is unacceptable.

The Guitarist and the Shrieking Fan Club

A guitarist once brought his own fan club to the venue. A group of young women took their seats near the front, there to cheer him on. At first, it seemed harmless enough — after all, every artist should have supporters in the room.

The problem began once the show started. One of them shrieked his name repeatedly, not once or twice, but throughout the performance. What might have been playful in another setting quickly became disruptive. The rest of the audience had come to enjoy a carefully curated evening of music. Instead, they were caught in a tug-of-war between the performance on stage and the interruptions in the room.

It wasn't cute. It wasn't supportive. It was a distraction that pulled the energy away from the music and left paying guests frustrated. My venue is not a high school gymnasium or an open mic night. It is a professional space where audiences expect artistry, not antics.

When I attempted to explain why her behavior was inappropriate, he was dismissive. He defended her actions and said he was simply thankful to have her in his corner. In that moment, it was clear that he valued her noise more than the experience of the rest of the room.

The guitarist may not have been the one shouting, but as the artist on stage, he carried responsibility for the atmosphere he brought with him.

By allowing the disruption to continue and then excusing it afterward, he showed a lack of awareness and leadership. The night was remembered not for his playing, but for the noise around it.

Professionalism means understanding that the experience belongs to everyone in the room, not just your fans.

The Singer Who Insulted the Crowd

She came highly recommended, referred by a respected musician I had worked with often. I trusted their word and booked her without previewing a show. Big mistake.

From the moment she stepped on stage, it was clear something was off. She did not sing so much as talk, and not in the charming, storyteller kind of way. Her remarks were odd, sometimes condescending, and a few bordered on offensive. Guests began shifting in their seats, glancing around, uncomfortable and unsure of what they had walked into. The energy in the room changed from anticipation to unease.

It was supposed to be a night of smooth vocals and good energy. Instead, it felt like a lecture no one asked for, delivered by someone who mistook sarcasm for style. By the time the show ended, guests were more relieved than entertained.

For over a year afterward, she called, texted, and emailed asking to return. But the best response I could give her was no response at all.

Some doors close quietly, and once they do, they stay closed.

The Renowned Saxophonist Who Affirmed the Standards

Mike Phillips, the internationally renowned saxophonist, has performed at Chayz Lounge several times. During one of his shows, he paused between songs and shared with the audience why he wanted to play at my venue.

He told them that he had read the glowing reviews, researched me, and was drawn to the intimacy of the space from the photos he had seen. He also said he had heard some not so good things about me from a few musicians. But knowing who those musicians were, he asked them a simple question: What did you not do right?

Then he went deeper. He told the room that women-owned jazz clubs are not common. That when you are a small business, a woman-owned business, and on top of that, a Black woman-owned business, you have to work three times as hard to maintain excellence. He reminded everyone that some musicians are not used to having their feet held to the fire, so instead of owning their mistakes, they blame the club owner or the booking agent.

Anyone but themselves.

He went on to say that his experience with me was refreshing compared to the countless venues he had worked with over the years. He told the audience he had been following me on social media for some time and chose to perform at Chayz Lounge not only to support a minority owned business, but also because he respected the values I displayed and the guidelines I had in place.

His words caught me off guard. For a brief moment, I became emotional. Because sometimes the fight to maintain standards feels like an uphill battle. To borrow the words of the late Moms Mabley, it was *"like trying to push a car up a hill—with a rope."*

And in that moment, to hear someone of Mike's caliber and his status affirm the very reasons behind those rules, reasons many others push back against, was both humbling and deeply validating.

That night, his music filled the room. But his words stayed with me long after the final note.

The Background Singer Who Took Over

A guitarist I had booked brought along a background singer I hadn't approved or even known about. That was the first red flag. During soundcheck, it became clear the background singer wasn't prepared. He didn't know the songs, seemed unsure of his parts, and looked visibly uncomfortable being in a supporting role. I pulled the guitarist aside and told him the singer didn't fit and shouldn't be part of the show. He agreed. That should've been the end of it.

It wasn't.

As the band headed to the stage, so did the background singer. I didn't want guests to witness a disruption, so I allowed him to perform, hoping for the best. It wasn't the best. There was an air about him, as if singing background was beneath him. The moment he got an opportunity to take a solo, he made it clear he had no intention of staying in the background. He strutted around the room, sang directly to women in the crowd, touched some of them, and made more than a few guests visibly uncomfortable with his behavior.

During the break, I saw him roaming the room as if it were his show. He was talking to tables, inserting himself into conversations, and acting like a headliner no one asked for. I pulled him aside, away from the guests, and calmly explained the expectations at Chayz Lounge. I asked him to tone it down.

He blew up. Loud, confrontational, and completely disrespectful. I had to ask him to leave. As he walked toward the exit, the air was thick with profanity. He even tried to slam the door in my face.

It was over a year before I allowed that guitarist back on my stage, and without the background singer.

Who you invite on stage reflects your judgment. If they are unprepared or unprofessional, their failure becomes yours. And when you bring someone in without the venue's approval, you break trust, which can cost you far more than a single show.

Arrogance Cancels Talent

A young musician once came to me seeking an opportunity. He was polite, seemed serious about his craft, and through several conversations with his mother, he impressed me as someone eager to perform on a professional stage. His communication was consistent, so I decided to give him a chance.

The night of the show, however, a very different young man arrived. He walked in with an air of arrogance, and the first thing he said was, *"I packed your house. I got a lot of people who want to see me play."* It was not just what he said, but the way he said it. He then began making demands: that tables be rearranged, the speakers swapped out for his own, and even that a plant that had been in the corner since our first meeting had to be removed because, in his words, *"it's ugly and it's gotta go."*

From the look on his mother's face, it seemed she was embarrassed. None of his demands were met. The show went on, and to his credit, he delivered a strong performance. But that night was both his first and last time on my stage. That was in 2017. I still have the plant, but I have no idea what became of that young man.

Talent may get you through the door, but arrogance will close it just as quickly. Venues remember character as much as performance, and no amount of skill can make up for disrespect.

The Singer Who Thought She Was the Star

She reached out to me after relocating to South Carolina, explaining that she used to perform in Hawaii but hadn't found a new home for her music. She sent videos of past performances, and I was impressed. There was potential there. I suggested she attend our Jazz After 5 series and sit in with the house band to build a following. And she did. About two months in, I was ready to give her a date for her first show.

I worked closely with her. Helped refine her stage presence. Offered guidance on improving her social media. We developed a set list, agreed on a fee, and since she didn't have any professional photos, I took some myself to create a flyer. Her debut show sold out.

When she arrived, her appearance was unexpected for someone so young. She wore a dowdy, oversized frock that looked more like something pulled from a closet than chosen for the stage. But I let it go. The real issue began once the music started. She forgot lyrics. Everything we had rehearsed about stage presence and performance style went out the window. She moved excessively, to the point where she became winded and had to take a break just thirty minutes into the show.

During the break, she changed the set list and the keys of several songs without notice. The second set didn't improve. Her voice cracked in multiple places and completely collapsed during a Whitney Houston song I had strongly advised her not to attempt.

After the show, the excuses came. The band was off. She was hot. She wasn't feeling her best. Nothing was her fault. A few days later, she called to book another show. I was still open to the idea until she demanded a higher fee. She explained that, beyond paying her babysitter, she felt she had earned it.

When I declined, she got upset and insisted the show was amazing, that the audience loved her, and that the only reason Chayz Lounge was packed was because of her. Then came the kicker. "Chayz Lounge is nothing without me." She claimed another venue owner had been in the audience and was ready to book her, so she didn't really need my stage.

We parted ways after that call. But she didn't stop there. She followed up with texts and emails declaring I had made a mistake, that I would regret not booking her, and that she was going to be huge. I expected to see her name on flyers across town.

I never did.

Two years later, she emailed me again. This time, she admitted she hadn't been able to get booked anywhere and asked for another chance. When I politely declined, the same ego returned.

I finally blocked her. ***Once you burn a bridge, the ashes are yours to carry.***

National Acts, Same Mistakes

It's not just newcomers who miss the mark. A few nationally known artists have found themselves uninvited to return. Not because of their talent, but because of their choices on stage. And when tickets are priced at a premium, expectations are just as high.

One act ended their set thirty minutes early without warning, leaving guests confused and disappointed. When I asked him to return to the stage, he declined, saying guests were leaving anyway.

Another went nearly an hour over their scheduled time, completely disrupting the flow of the evening and pushing my staff into unexpected overtime.

Then there were the artists who brought in sound so loud and overpowering, it shifted the ambiance of Chayz Lounge from a curated listening experience to something closer to a nightclub.

When you're a known act, the bar isn't lower. It's higher. People come with expectations. The experience has to match the price and the promise.

The Drummer Who Chose Not to See Me

Every now and then, someone walks into my venue and makes it clear without saying a word that they do not see me. Not because they did not notice me or my staff, but because they chose not to acknowledge us.

One night, a national act was scheduled to perform. I had booked the headliner directly, but she brought in a drummer through a referral. I did not know him. He was not part of my usual rotation.

He arrived early. Walked through the room, looked straight at me, and kept walking. No hello. No nod. Just silence as he headed to the stage. Back and forth he went, hauling drum cases, never once speaking to me or my staff. I noticed. I tucked it away.

Then the headliner arrived.

Suddenly, the same drummer who could not spare me a hello was grinning ear to ear. All smiles. Eager energy.

"Yes, Miss ____."
"I will get that for you, Miss ____."

He was attentive, talkative, completely deferential.

In the normal course of pre-show prep I asked him a direct question; he ignored me. He turned to the headliner instead, asking what "she" needed him to do. The shift was blatant, the disrespect deliberate. It rubbed me the wrong way.

He was Black.
The headliner was White.

I could not ignore the contrast. He moved with respect and sweetness toward her, while treating me with casual, but conscious disregard. In his mind I did not warrant a response unless it came through her.

I understood that being a female venue owner was rare. Being a Black female venue owner, even more so. I had faced challenges with male musicians before, but this was the first time I felt my gender and my race dismissed in real time.

During the break, I approached him about having an open drink on stage. He snapped and that is when the volcano erupted. He told me I had no business addressing him now since I had not spoken to him earlier. Then came the résumé. He rattled off the big-name artists he had played with, as if that excused his behavior. I did not engage. I walked away.

After the show, I tried again, calmly, to address his tone and disrespect. He blew up a second time, louder. According to him, I was just another "bitch with an attitude."

Noticing the exchange, the headliner walked over, and then just like before, his entire demeanor shifted. He softened. His voice lowered. He became sweet, even self-deprecating, and told her I was the problem. That I had disrespected him.

I stood there and watched it unfold. Watched the performance behind the performance.

That is when I decided to say what needed to be said.

"You had no issue addressing her the moment she walked in. You rushed to carry her bags. But you did not think I was worth a hello. Was it because she is white and I am a black woman who you did not think you had to answer to?"

The room went quiet, the atmosphere tense. The headliner stood silent. He did not respond, all the sudden at a loss for words to my direct ask. And I doubt she knew what to say.

About a year later, another musician tried to bring him in as their drummer. When I said no and explained why, they had no trouble finding a replacement.

If you cannot extend basic respect to the person running the room, especially when she looks like you, then you do not deserve the privilege of that stage. Titles do not excuse you. Referrals do not protect you. And your résumé means nothing if you fail to check your "baggage" at the door.

The Saxophonist Who Became Family

There is a musician my staff refers to as their favorite saxophonist. David Glymph is that person. He has been another one of my go-to musicians since before I opened the doors of Chayz Lounge, back when I was producing shows at different venues to build my reputation and brand. From the very beginning, David set himself apart with his humility, professionalism, versatility, and dedication to his craft.

There were times, especially in the early years, when shows did not turn out to be as financially beneficial as I had hoped. On those occasions, David voluntarily accepted less pay, and at times he even forgave his fee altogether. Not because he did not need the money, but because he believed in me, my vision, and what I was building. That level of support spoke volumes.

The entire staff lights up whenever they know David is scheduled to perform, and for good reason. He is genuinely kind, he always delivers a phenomenal performance, and he consistently shows respect for both the venue and the people who make it run. He cares deeply about the guests and makes it his goal to ensure they receive the quality show they paid for.

At my venue, every guest purchases a ticket to attend. They come expecting an experience, not background music. David understands that when guests are enjoying themselves, their mood and energy improve, which in turn makes the staff's job easier and often results in larger tips. On top of all that, he never leaves without tipping the servers himself. That simple gesture does not go unnoticed. It reflects gratitude, respect, and an understanding of the bigger picture.

David has been consistently professional and dedicated from the beginning, and he continues to be that today. His commitment to entertaining his audience, coupled with his character, has made him one of my most trusted musicians. To me and my staff, he is more than an artist I book. He is family. His belief in me from day one deserves to be etched in this book.

True professionalism goes beyond talent. Humility, consistency, and belief in something greater than yourself build bonds that last. Those qualities turn gigs into partnerships and musicians into family.

The Hip-Hop Detour

The band had been a regular part of my lineup for some time. Reliable. Well rehearsed. So when the bandleader asked if she could bring in two male vocalists for a specific night, I didn't question it. She had earned a level of trust.

That trust dissolved quickly.

The vocalists were introduced mid-set. They weren't great. Pitchy, off rhythm, and clearly unprepared. Still, I was willing to let it slide and chalk it up to a poor decision in judgment.

But then the set took a hard left turn. The musicians stopped playing. They cued up backing tracks. Suddenly we had gone from a soul experience to full-on hip hop mode.
It wasn't subtle. It wasn't requested. And it wasn't remotely what I expected, would have approved, or what the audience had come for. The lead vocalist danced along with the music, smiling as if all was well.

Many guests were visibly thrown off, and some left early. That band hasn't been back on my stage since.

Just like that, the stellar relationship that had been built over years was shattered beyond repair. Trust, once broken, cannot be regained.

The Saxophonist Who Walked Off Mid-Show

This particular artist had performed at Chayz Lounge for three years straight. The Lounge was a guaranteed stop on his routing. He was talented, courteous, professional, easygoing off stage, and reliable enough to keep booking. Over time, I came to know his tendencies. He had a specific way he liked things done, especially when it came to sound. If the monitor mix wasn't dialed in just right, he would voice his concerns. Not rudely, but always with the tone of someone used to getting what he wanted, especially when speaking to the musicians.

That night, everything started as expected. Soundcheck went smoothly. He signed off on the mix and gave me a nod of approval. The room was full, the energy was warm, and the band launched into their set. About thirty minutes into the show, he stopped playing. No signal to the band. No explanation. He lowered his horn and walked off the stage to find me.

At first, people thought it might be part of the performance, maybe a solo exit or some theatrical moment. It wasn't. The band scrambled to fill the space. The crowd looked around, puzzled. The energy we had worked hard to build began to crack.

He approached me, irritated. Said the monitor mix wasn't clear enough and claimed he couldn't perform under those conditions. I reminded him that everything had been fine during soundcheck, but he wasn't trying to hear it. He doubled down and got defensive. Eventually, he returned to the stage, but the vibe in the room was already lost.

About a week after the show, he called to set a return date. I calmly explained that the way he handled the sound issue was unprofessional, and that the audience should never be made aware of problems on stage. He didn't take the feedback well. He also wasn't interested in hearing that his setlist had become predictable. The next day, he unfriended me on social media.

That situation taught me something simple but unforgettable. ***No matter how many years you've worked with someone, if they can walk off stage mid-show, they were never really there for the experience to begin with. And if they're not open to feedback, they'll never grow.***

I can say with certainty that his feet will never make their way to my stage again.

The Musicians Who Got Too Comfortable

There is a certain familiarity that forms over time, especially with musicians who have been with me for years. It is natural. But sometimes, that familiarity turns into something else: complacency.

When that happens, they stop trying. They stop dressing the part. They stop showing up with energy. On stage, they look bored, as if they would rather be anywhere else. They forget that they are being paid not just to play music, but to entertain and create an experience for the guests.

I have pulled them aside. I have had conversations. I have encouraged them to do better. But nothing changes. At some point, professionalism fades and entitlement takes over.

When that happens, I do not make a scene. I simply stop hiring them.

Complacency is the enemy of longevity.

The Musician Who Became a Go-To

Charles Page is one of those rare musicians every venue owner hopes to work with. He not only comes prepared with a fresh set, but he always arrives on time, carries himself with professionalism, shows respect for the room, and consistently delivers a performance our guests love. He has become a favorite, and with good reason.

Charles is also there in a pinch. On occasions when a booked musician failed to show, if Charles was free, he made his way to the lounge, on a moment's notice, from a neighboring state, to save the night. That kind of reliability is priceless in this business.

And in an era where chivalry often feels like a dying art, Charles proves otherwise. I recall one evening when a man wandered into the venue mid-show and posed a visible threat. Before I could react, Charles was off the stage, gently escorting the man out of the building. He then returned to finish the performance as if nothing had happened. That moment spoke volumes about his character and presence.

Charles understands what it means to honor the room. He respects the staff, values the guests, and treats every performance as if it matters, because it does. He makes my job easier, and he elevates the reputation of the stage every time he plays it.

That is what longevity looks like.

Soundcheck Is Not Rehearsal

This happens more often than it should. One musician in particular stands out. He and his band always arrive on time, set up quickly, and begin their soundcheck in record time. Everything goes along fine until it does not.

Once the levels are set, I ask him to stop. But he always asks for "just a few more minutes" and continues playing. Full songs. Rehearsing as if it were a private concert. It always seems to surprise him when I use a firm tone. More than once, I have had to remind him that if the band does not know the song by now, they are not going to learn it in the five minutes he is asking for.

Our doors open at 6:30 PM, and the contract clearly states that soundcheck must be completed by 6:00. Yet he often pushes it right up to the moment guests begin walking into the space. The polished atmosphere we worked hard to create shifts instantly to unprofessional, and guests feel it.

Soundcheck is for levels. It is not a rehearsal, nor is it a practice session. Professionalism starts before the first note.

He demands professional payment but conducts himself like a regular gigging musician. His last performance at Chayz Lounge was his last performance on my stage.

Payment and professionalism go hand in hand. You cannot demand one while neglecting the other.

The Musician Who Blamed Me for His Mistakes

A musician once reached out about performing at Chayz Lounge. It was a duo with him and another artist. I did my research, both checked all the boxes, so I booked them. The contract was sent, signed, and returned promptly.

Leading up to the performance, he asked all the right questions and arrived on time for soundcheck. Everything appeared to be in order until it wasn't.

At 8:10, ten minutes after the show was scheduled to begin, the duo returned to the venue. I pulled him aside to ask why he was late. His response stunned me. He said he had to find a hotel. I explained that I do not believe in keeping my guests waiting and that our shows always start on time. He blew up and told me his tardiness was my fault because I had not booked his hotel.

I was taken aback. The contract clearly stated that he was responsible for his own accommodations, transportation to and from the venue, as well as food and beverages. By signing it, he had agreed to those terms. None of that mattered to him. He went on to claim that he knew for a fact I provided those things for other artists, and because I had failed to do the same for him, they were forced to stay in a cheap motel.

The other half of the duo did his best to de-escalate the situation, but the outburst continued.

Rather than argue, I reminded him of what he had signed and told him he should have read the contract for understanding before agreeing to it. I ended the exchange, walked to the stage, and introduced the band and the headliners, which signaled to them that it was time to take their place.

The show itself went on and the music was good, but that artist was never invited back. His partner, however, proved himself professional, and I have booked him several times since.

Opportunities demand accountability. Contracts are not suggestions, they are agreements. They exist for clarity and fairness, but they only work if they are read and understood.

Professionalism begins long before stepping on stage, and it starts with honoring what you have signed. If something in a contract is unfamiliar, the time to ask questions is before signing, not after failing to meet expectations.

An artist who neglects this responsibility risks more than confusion. They risk their credibility. Venue owners and booking agents notice the difference between those who take responsibility and those who cast blame. One will always be welcomed back. The other will not.

Overpromising and Overstepping

I once booked a nationally recognized musician who had already disappointed me by overpromising and failing to fill a room of 60 seats, not once but twice. That alone damaged his credibility. But what happened next made matters worse.

He brought his elderly father to the show. At first the man was polite, but after two drinks he became loud, obnoxious, and overly forward with my female staff. I pulled him aside and spoke firmly to keep the situation under control. After the show, I raised the matter with the headliner. That was when he told me we should never have served his father because he had a drinking problem. He admitted that his father may have arrived already intoxicated, which explained how quickly the alcohol hit him.

As an artist, you are responsible for the people you bring into the venue. If a guest you invite disrupts the staff or the audience, it reflects on you and can cost you future opportunities. Overpromising and underdelivering is damaging enough, but coupling that with poor judgment about who you bring with you is a career killer.

The Guitarist Who Played for Himself

He was a last-minute selection, booked to fill in for a
canceled act. He couldn't pull his full band together in time
but offered to perform solo, assuring me that neither I nor
the guests would be disappointed. He arrived on time, was
respectful, and came prepared. On the surface, everything
was in place.

But as the night went on, something was missing. I kept
waiting for a familiar tune. Something the audience could
latch onto. A melody they could hum. A rhythm that would
get the room swaying. It never came.

He played only original material. And while he was clearly
talented, no one in the audience seemed to connect, because
they didn't know the songs. There was no invitation into the
music. At one point, I looked over and saw him sitting in a
chair. Legs crossed. Guitar in his lap. Head back. Eyes
closed. Strumming and tapping his feet. Lost in his own
rhythm. Oblivious to the guests in front of him, or the ones
quietly getting up to leave.

To his credit, he was receptive when I offered feedback. He
didn't argue. He didn't make excuses. He listened. He even
thanked me. And nearly a decade later, I still remember his
name, when I've forgotten many others. Not because of his
performance, but because of his humility and openness to
growth.

The only reason he wasn't invited back is because I later learned that his repertoire was limited, and that night reflected the full extent of what he could offer musically.

Humility will be remembered long after the music fades. And unless you are a legend in the industry with a catalog of hit songs, packing a set with only original material is not the way to go.

The Reminder of Why... Malcolm-Jamal Warner

The first time I met Malcolm-Jamal Warner, he arrived early, before I even reached the venue. He was already on stage, tuning his bass guitar. When I walked in, he looked up, smiled, and greeted me as if we had known each other all our lives. I was immediately struck by his genuine warmth and humility. For someone of his caliber and status to be so down to earth was unexpected and beyond refreshing. He was courteous to the staff, professional in every way, and never once questioned a single house rule.

Every so often, I think back to the reason I opened the doors of Chayz Lounge: to bring music lovers together with some of the finest talents in the world, and more than that, to give people the opportunity to experience icons up close and personal. I have been fortunate to fulfill that vision, as remarkable artists such as Melba Moore, Nils, TC Carson, Tom Browne, Jeff Lorber, Bob Baldwin, Meli'sa Morgan, Anthony David, Chandra Currelley, and Malcolm-Jamal Warner have graced my stage. Each one honored the room, respected the stage, and shared their artistry masterfully.

There have been times when that mission felt distant, and moments when I considered walking away. Yet something always pulls me back—a message from a guest, a word of encouragement from an artist, or an evening like the ones Malcolm created for us.

He did not merely perform. He commanded the stage and left an imprint. His magnetism, storytelling, and the way he captivated the audience held us all in awe.

Malcolm-Jamal Warner performed at Chayz Lounge twice, and each time he raised the bar for anyone who would follow. More than that, his conversations were as enlightening as his music and poetry, and he encouraged me to keep going, affirming the importance of the space I created.

To say it was a pleasure to have known him would be an understatement.

His presence will forever live in my memory.

The Musicians Who Earned the Return

I could easily write a book filled with my less-than-positive encounters with some musicians. But the truth is, the good outweighs the bad. In my 30-plus years in the music industry, I've had the pleasure of meeting and working with countless notable talents such as TLC, Boyz II Men, Angela Bofill, Jody Watley, Sheryl Lee Ralph, and other previously mentioned icons. My experience with them has been nothing like the negative encounters I've shared here.

There are musicians I may not have written about who have graced my stage, some more frequently than others, yet each leaves a lasting impression and shows genuine care and respect for Chayz Lounge. They deserve recognition.

Saxophonist Jeanette Harris, whose sound radiates joy and uplifts the entire space. Flautist Kim Scott, whose expressive playing flows with warmth and precision. Guitarist JJ Sansaverino, whose passion for both his craft and his audience shines through every chord. Flautist Ragan Whiteside, whose stage presence captivates from the first breath of her flute. Saxophonist Paula Atherton, whose vibrant performances blend technical mastery with a joy that fills the room.

Alongside these remarkable artists are performers from our region and neighboring states who travel in, deliver outstanding shows, and remind guests why the drive is always worth it. Some you may see more often than others, but all share the same commitment to excellence.
Among them are Violinist JaVonne Jones, whose soulful artistry transforms every note into an experience. Singer Brittany Turnipseed, whose angelic voice lingers in the heart long after the last note. H. Wade Johnson, whose boundless

energy gets the audience doing far more than tapping their feet. Letron Brantley & Friends, whose dynamic arrangements turn every set into a soul-stirring celebration. Jamie Wright, whose rich, versatile voice and engaging stage presence create unforgettable evenings of classic and contemporary soul. Connie Sawyer, whose warm saxophone tone and effortless delivery bring elegance to the stage. Bassist Bryan Anderson, whose deep grooves and seasoned band craft nights of sophisticated R&B and jazz. Willie Walker & Conversation Piece, whose tight musicianship and infectious energy keep audiences moving from start to finish. Reggie Graves & Jazz Theory, whose intricate guitar work and inspired improvisations blend contemporary jazz with classic soul grooves. Guitarist Rod Harris Jr., whose soul-stirring fusion of R&B, smooth jazz, hip-hop, and funk creates a groove that captivates every audience.

What all of these musicians share in common is an understanding. They recognize that our guidelines are not restrictions but a framework designed to ensure the best experience for paying guests and the smooth operation of the business. They respect that every detail matters.

So when you see names repeated on my lineup of upcoming shows, know that it is because these musicians have earned their place on my stage. More importantly, they have earned the return.

Closing Thoughts

As I reflect on the stories and lessons in these pages, one truth stands clear: this business is about far more than music. It is about integrity, respect, and professionalism. The stage is sacred, and every performance carries weight.

Yes, there have been artists who missed the mark, and those stories carry valuable lessons for anyone pursuing a career in music. But the real joy lies in the many who rise to the occasion, walk through our doors prepared and humble, and honor both their craft and the audience. They are the reason I opened Chayz Lounge and the reason I continue to nurture this space.

Talent may open doors, but character is what keeps them open. To every musician reading this, remember that venues are not just places to play; they are homes for experiences. When you respect the stage, the staff, the guests, and yourself, you earn more than a booking. You build a career with staying power and truly earn the return.

Acknowledgments

This book would not have been possible without the musicians who brought both their best and their worst to the stage. To those who stood with me through the trying times, including the pandemic, and shared in the joyful moments, thank you. Every encounter, positive or otherwise, has been a lesson worth sharing.

I am deeply grateful to the guests of Chayz Lounge, whose presence and feedback remind me why I do this work. Some of you have become more than patrons. You have become friends whom I cherish.

To Kim Boxley, my chief cheerleader whose support has been unwavering for nearly two decades and whose belief in me is at times greater than my own, thank you.

To Roi Canty, who began as a guest and is now a close friend, thank you for being my sounding board, for providing valuable feedback, and for your continued support.

To my dedicated staff at Chayz Lounge, thank you for holding the line, protecting the standard and the brand, and making every night a success. I may do a lot, but your work ensures every guest leaves with a memorable experience.

About the Author

Chaye Alexander is the visionary and brand architect of Chayz Lounge, Columbia's boutique destination for live jazz and dining. She is also the creator of Chayz Lounge Radio, a 24/7 streaming station blending smooth jazz with soulful sophistication.

With Chayz Lounge, Chaye has redefined hospitality, not as service but as a feeling. The venue embodies her Sophisti-Soul philosophy: Curated Moments. Soulful Sounds. Elevated Experiences. Every detail is designed to create moments that linger long after the last note fades. Over the years, she has also presented some of the most notable names in jazz and soul, curating unforgettable moments for audiences.

Chaye's influence extends beyond the Lounge. Chaye serves the arts community as Musical Director for the Columbia Museum of Art's *Live at Boyd Plaza* Concert Series and the Richland County Parks and Recreation Foundation's *Jazz Fest*. She also serves on the board of the South Carolina Jazz Foundation and is the visionary behind West Columbia's *Meeting Street Music Fest*, helping to foster a vibrant and enduring music culture within the community.

Connect with Chaye Alexander

To learn more about my work, upcoming projects, and the experiences I curate at Chayz Lounge, visit:

ChayzLounge.com

ChayeAlexander.com

You can also find my reflections and creative work at:

Chayeology.substack.com

www.ingramcontent.com/pod-product-compliance
Lightning Source LLC
Chambersburg PA
CBHW051641120626
46551CB00014B/2169